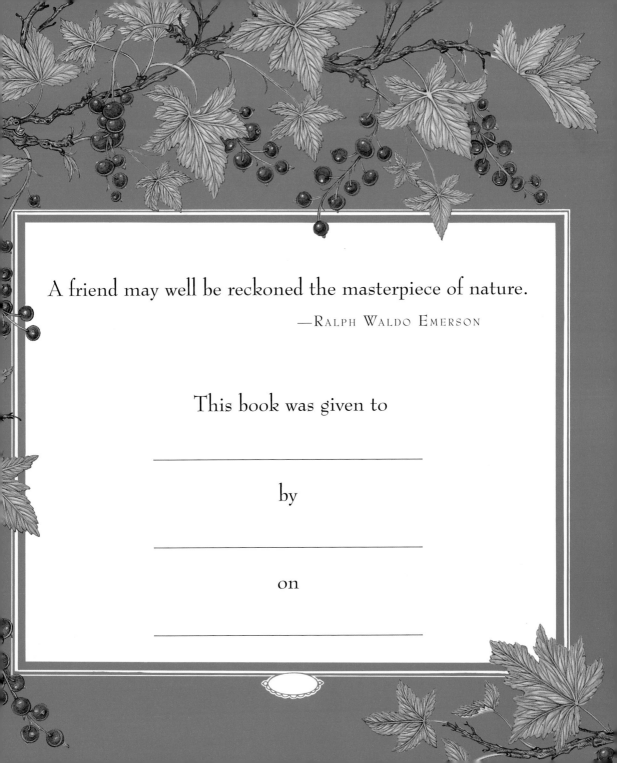

A friend may well be reckoned the masterpiece of nature.

—RALPH WALDO EMERSON

This book was given to

_____

by

_____

on

_____

KINDRED SPIRITS

Meditations on Family and Friends

Paintings by Claudia Karabaic Sargent
Edited by Peg Streep

VIKING
STUDIO
BOOKS

For my family, with all my love: my parents, Georgia and Anton;
my sisters and brothers-in-law, Janet and Walter, Nancy and Chris, Barbara and George; my brother and
sister-in-law, John and Cheryl; my nieces, Amanda
and Alyssa; my mother-in-law, Irene; and my best friends and true loves,
my husband, Frank, and Rowfa

—C. K. S.

For Alexandra, kin, and Peter, kind, and for all of my friends,
but especially Erika

—P. S.

VIKING STUDIO BOOKS
Published by the Penguin Group
Penguin Books USA Inc.,
375 Hudson Street, New York, New York 10014, U.S.A.
Penguin Books Ltd, 27 Wrights Lane, London W8 5TZ, England
Penguin Books Australia Ltd, Ringwood, Victoria, Australia
Penguin Books Canada Ltd, 10 Alcorn Avenue, Toronto, Ontario, Canada M4V 3B2
Penguin Books (N.Z.) Ltd, 182–190 Wairau Road, Auckland 10, New Zealand

Penguin Books Ltd, Registered Offices:
Harmondsworth, Middlesex, England

First published in 1995 by Viking Penguin, a division of Penguin Books USA Inc.

1 3 5 7 9 10 8 6 4 2

LIBRARY OF CONGRESS CATALOGING IN PUBLICATION DATA
Kindred Spirits: meditations on family and friends / paintings by
Claudia Karabaic Sargent : edited by Peg Streep.
p. cm.
ISBN 0-670-85436-0
1. Family—Quotations, maxims, etc. 2. Friendship—Quotations,
maxims, etc. I. Sargent, Claudia Karabaic. II. Streep, Peg.
PN6084.F23K56 1995
082—dc20   94-151658

Printed in Japan
Set in Bernhard Modern
Designed by Kathryn Parise

Preface

The word *kindred* illuminates some of the most important verities about family and friends, for the family of words it belongs to includes *kind* and *kindness* as well as *kin*. In its narrowest meaning, *kindred* applies only to those we are connected to by blood: our parents and their parents, our siblings, and our children. Not even husbands and wives fit this definition; the relationships of *kin* are ruled by birth alone and are beyond choice.

Figuratively, though, *kindred* means to have a shared affinity or affinities, quality or qualities, a common point of character or connection. Here, *kindred* describes the relationships we choose for ourselves: friends, lovers, husbands, wives. If we are supremely graced and also lucky, the two meanings of *kindred* overlap, and we find in our mother or father, sister or brother, daughter or son, the kindred spirits we would have chosen.

The meditations and reflections in *Kindred Spirits* explore the complexities and contradictions, the joy and pain, of these two kinds of relationships. Its four sections, "Discovery," "Sustenance," "Changes," and "Love," seek to reveal, in words and images, the range of human feeling involved in our struggles to connect and maintain connection with others throughout life. "Discovery" etches the truths and perceptions that emerge from our experiences of family and friends. "Sustenance" sets before us the myriad ways in which the hands of others steady us on the path that is life. "Changes" reveals, paradoxically, that the very strength of these ties may lie in their fragility and that we must honor what we value most. "Love" reminds us of the extraordinary blessing conferred upon us by others and that, in reaching out, we reach inside as well.

We have chosen the words of the American poet Walt Whitman to unify this volume of meditations, for his work tells us he knew well the essential kindred spirit beneath the visible differences in all the denizens of the planet—women, men, and children alike.

—Peg Streep

Contents

Passing Stranger! you do not know how longingly I look upon you,
   You must be he I was seeking, or she I was seeking, (it comes to me as of a
      dream,)
   I have somewhere surely lived a life of joy with you . . .
   I am not to speak to you, I am to think of you when I sit alone or wake at night
      alone,
   I am to wait, I do not doubt I am to meet you again,
   I am to see to it that I do not lose you.

—WALT WHITMAN

Discovery

We make ourselves a place apart
    Behind light words that tease and flout,
But oh, the agitated heart
    Till someone really find us out.

'Tis pity if the case require
    (Or so we say) that in the end
We speak the literal to inspire
    The understanding of a friend.

14

But so with all, from babes that play
　　At hide-and-seek to God afar,
So all who hide too well away
　　Must speak and tell us where they are.

—ROBERT FROST

$\mathcal{W}$hat is a friend?
A single soul
dwelling in two
bodies.

—ARISTOTLE

16

One fact the fine conversations of the last week—now already fast fading into oblivion—revealed to me, not without a certain shudder of joy, that I must thank what I am, and not what I do, for the love my friends bear me. I, conscious all the time of the short-comings of my hands, haunted ever with a sense of beauty which makes all I do and say pitiful to me, and the occasion of perpetual apologies, assure myself to disgust those whom I admire,—and now suddenly it comes out that they have been loving me all the time, not thinking of my hands or my words, but only of that love of something more beautiful than the world, which, it seems, being in my heart, overflowed through my eyes or the tones of my speech.

—Ralph Waldo Emerson

17

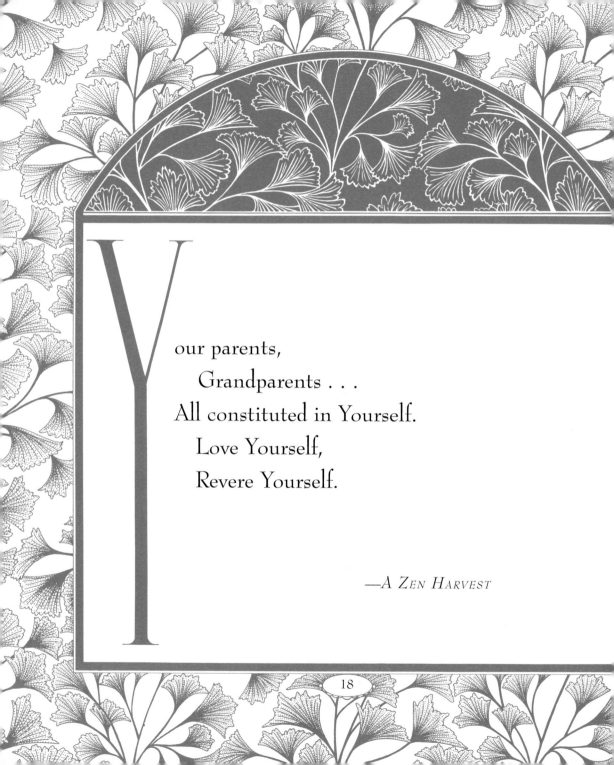

Your parents,
    Grandparents . . .
All constituted in Yourself.
    Love Yourself,
    Revere Yourself.

—*A Zen Harvest*

18

The most important sphere of giving, however, is not that of material things, but lies in the specifically human realm. What does one person give to another? He gives of himself, of the most precious he has, he gives of his life. This does not necessarily mean that he sacrifices his life for the other—but that he gives him of that which is alive in him; he gives him of his joy, of his interest, of his understanding, of his knowledge, of his humor, of his sadness—of all expressions and manifestations of that which is alive in him. In thus giving of his life, he enriches the other person, he enhances the other's sense of aliveness by enhancing his own sense of aliveness. He does not give in order to receive; giving is in itself exquisite joy. But in giving he cannot help bringing something to life in the other person, and this which is brought to life reflects back to him; in truly giving, he cannot help receiving that which is given back to him. Giving implies to make the other person a giver also and they both share in the joy of what they have brought to life. In the act of giving something is born, and both persons involved are grateful for the life that is born for both of them.

—ERICH FROMM

19

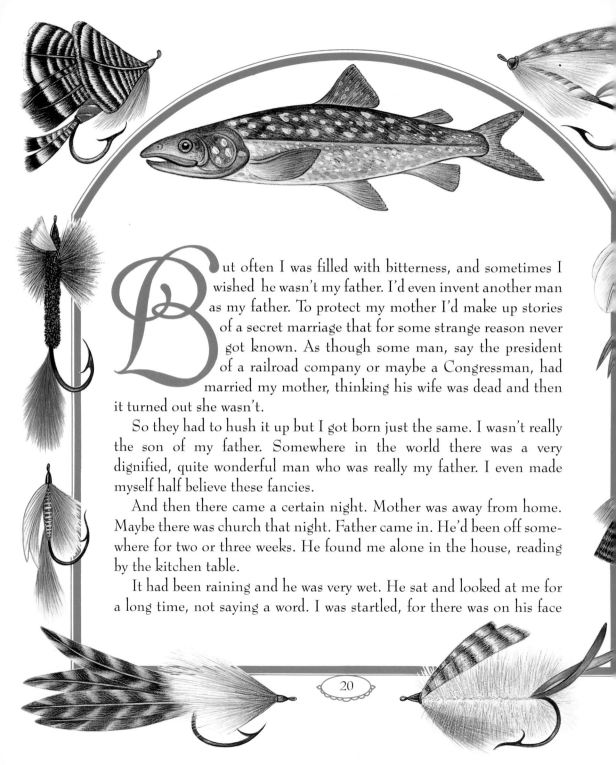

ut often I was filled with bitterness, and sometimes I wished he wasn't my father. I'd even invent another man as my father. To protect my mother I'd make up stories of a secret marriage that for some strange reason never got known. As though some man, say the president of a railroad company or maybe a Congressman, had married my mother, thinking his wife was dead and then it turned out she wasn't.

So they had to hush it up but I got born just the same. I wasn't really the son of my father. Somewhere in the world there was a very dignified, quite wonderful man who was really my father. I even made myself half believe these fancies.

And then there came a certain night. Mother was away from home. Maybe there was church that night. Father came in. He'd been off somewhere for two or three weeks. He found me alone in the house, reading by the kitchen table.

It had been raining and he was very wet. He sat and looked at me for a long time, not saying a word. I was startled, for there was on his face

the saddest look I had ever seen. He sat for a time, his clothes dripping.
Then he got up.

"Come on with me," he said.

I got up and went with him out of the house. I was filled with wonder
but I wasn't afraid. We went along a dirt road that led into a valley, about
a mile out of town, where there was a pond. We walked in silence. The
man who was always talking had stopped his talking.

I didn't know what was up and had the queer feeling that I was with
a stranger. I didn't know whether my father intended it so. I don't think
he did.

The pond was quite large. It was still raining hard and there
were flashes of lightning followed by thunder. We were on a grassy
bank at the pond's edge when my father spoke, and in the
darkness and rain his voice sounded strange.

"Take off your clothes," he said. Still filled with wonder, I began
to undress. There was a flash of lightning and I saw that he was already
naked.

Naked, we went into the pond. Taking my hand, he pulled me in.

21

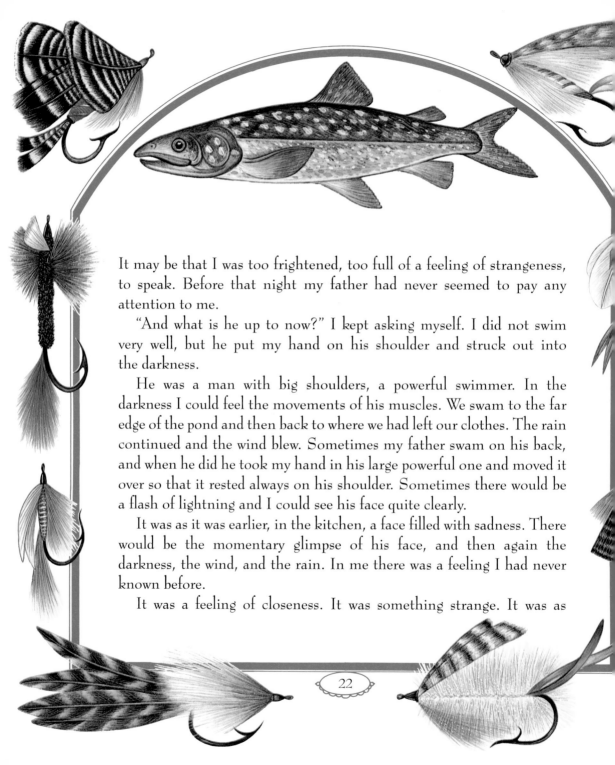

It may be that I was too frightened, too full of a feeling of strangeness, to speak. Before that night my father had never seemed to pay any attention to me.

"And what is he up to now?" I kept asking myself. I did not swim very well, but he put my hand on his shoulder and struck out into the darkness.

He was a man with big shoulders, a powerful swimmer. In the darkness I could feel the movements of his muscles. We swam to the far edge of the pond and then back to where we had left our clothes. The rain continued and the wind blew. Sometimes my father swam on his back, and when he did he took my hand in his large powerful one and moved it over so that it rested always on his shoulder. Sometimes there would be a flash of lightning and I could see his face quite clearly.

It was as it was earlier, in the kitchen, a face filled with sadness. There would be the momentary glimpse of his face, and then again the darkness, the wind, and the rain. In me there was a feeling I had never known before.

It was a feeling of closeness. It was something strange. It was as

though there were only we two in the world. It was though I had been jerked suddenly out of myself, out of my world of the schoolboy, out of a world in which I was ashamed of my father.

He had become blood of my blood; he the strong swimmer and I the boy clinging to him in the darkness. We swam in silence, and in the silence we dressed in our wet clothes and went home.

There was a lamp lighted in the kitchen, and when we came in, the water dripping from us, there was my mother. She smiled at us. I remember that she called us "boys." "What have you boys been up to?" she asked, but my father did not answer. As he had begun the evening's experience with me in silence, so he ended it. He turned and looked at me. Then he went, I thought, with a new and strange dignity, out of the room.

I climbed the stairs to my room, undressed in the darkness and got into bed. I couldn't sleep and did not want to sleep. For the first time I knew that I was the son of my father. He was a storyteller as I was to be. It may be that I even laughed a little softly there in the darkness. If I did, I laughed knowing that I would never again be wanting another father.

—SHERWOOD ANDERSON

23

I was sitting on a beach one summer day, watching two children, a boy and a girl, playing in the sand. They were hard at work building an elaborate sand castle by the water's edge, with gates and towers and moats and internal passages. Just when they had nearly finished their project, a big wave came along and knocked it down, reducing it to a heap of wet sand. I expected the children to burst into tears, devastated by what had happened to all their hard work. But they surprised me. Instead, they ran up the shore away from the water, laughing and holding hands, and sat down to build another castle. I realized that they had taught me an important lesson. All the things in our lives, all the complicated structures we spend so much time and energy creating, are built on sand. Only our relationships to other people endure. Sooner or later, the wave will come along and knock down what we have worked so hard to build up. When that happens, only the person who has somebody's hand to hold will be able to laugh.

—HAROLD S. KUSHNER

Your voice, my friend,
   wanders in my heart,
   like the muffled sound of the sea
   among the listening pines.

—RABINDRANATH TAGORE

And a youth said, Speak to us of Friendship.

And he answered, saying:

Your friend is your needs answered.

He is your field which you sow with love and reap with thanksgiving.

And he is your board and your fireside.

For you come to him with your hunger, and you seek him for peace.

When your friend speaks his mind you fear not the "nay" in your own mind, nor do you withhold the "ay."

And when he is silent your heart ceases not to listen to his heart;

For without words, in friendship, all thoughts, all desires, all expectations are born and shared, with joy that is unacclaimed.

When you part from your friend, you grieve not;

For that which you love most in him may be clearer in his absence, as the

mountain to the climber is clearer from the plain.

And let there be no purpose in friendship save the deepening of the spirit.

For love that seeks aught but the disclosure of its own mystery is not love but a net cast forth: and only the unprofitable is caught.

And let your best be for your friend.

If he must know the ebb of your tide, let him know its flood also.

For what is your friend that you should seek him with hours to kill?

Seek him always with hours to live.

For it is his to fill your need, but not your emptiness.

And in the sweetness of friendship let there be laughter, and sharing of pleasures.

For in the dew of little things the heart finds its morning and is refreshed.

—KAHLIL GIBRAN

"What do you think it was that made you decide to devote your life to art?" a friend once asked me. . . .

The question sent my thoughts wandering back through the past for an answer until they stopped before the tiny figure of myself when I was about six years old. I had been out in the garden playing with the flowers. The colors evidently stirred something latent in me for I can remember, as distinctly as though it had happened yesterday, the feeling of intense excitement that swept over me and carried me into the house and up to my grandmother. . . .

"How did they ever get these

beautiful colors?" I demanded breathlessly, holding a small bunch of flowers out towards her.

She put out her hand and touched me and then the flowers—for she had been blind for many years—and very solemnly and impressively explained that colors were given flowers by God.

"He painted them!" I gasped.

She nodded, still very solemn.

"How?"

At this she laid down her knitting and her voice came a bit uneasily. "Why do you ask that, my child?"

"Because I want to paint some just like them. I've got to! I must!"

—JANET SCUDDER

The relation of two sisters is not that of a man and a woman. But it can illustrate the essence of relationships. The light shed by any good relationship illuminates all relationships. And one perfect day can give clues for a more perfect life—the mythical life, maybe, of the argonauta.

We wake in the same small room from the deep sleep of good children, to the soft sound of wind through the casuarina trees and the gentle sleep-breathing rhythm of waves on the shore. We run bare-legged to the beach, which lies smooth, flat, and glistening with fresh wet shells after the night's tides. The morning swim has the nature of a blessing to me, a baptism, a rebirth to the beauty and wonder of the world. We run back tingling to hot coffee on our small back porch. Two kitchen chairs and a child's table between us fill the stoop on which we sit. With legs in the sun we laugh and plan our day.

We wash the dishes lightly to no system, for there are not enough to matter. We work easily and instinctively together, not bumping into each other as we go back and forth about our tasks. We talk as we sweep, as we dry, as we put away, discussing a person or a poem or a memory. And since our communication seems more important to us than our chores, the chores are done without thinking.

And then to work, behind closed doors neither of us would want to invade. What release to write so that one forgets oneself, forgets one's companion, forgets where one is or what one is going to do next—to be drenched in work as one is drenched in sleep or in the sea. Pencils and pads and curling blue sheets alive with letters heap up on the desk. And then, pricked by hunger, we rise at last in a daze, for a late lunch. Reeling a little from our intense absorption, we come back with relief to our small chores of getting lunch, as if they were lifelines to reality—as if we had indeed almost drowned in the sea of intellectual work and welcomed the firm ground of physical action under our feet.

After an hour or so of practical jobs and errands we are ready to leave them again. Out onto the beach for the afternoon where we are swept clean of duties, of the particular, of the practical. We walk up the beach in silence, but in harmony, as the sandpipers ahead of us move like a corps of ballet dancers keeping time to some interior rhythm inaudible to us. Intimacy is blown away. Emotions are carried out to sea. We are even free of thoughts, at least of their articulation; clean and bare as whitened driftwood; empty as shells, ready to be filled up again with the impersonal sea and sky and wind. A long afternoon soaking up the outer world.

And when we are heavy and relaxed as the seaweed under our feet, we return at dusk to the warmth and intimacy of our cottage. We sip sherry at leisure in front of a fire. We start supper and we talk. Evening is the time for conversation. Morning is for mental work, I feel, the habit of school-days persisting in me. Afternoon is for physical tasks, the out-of-door jobs. But evening is for sharing, for communication. Is it the uninterrupted dark expanse of the night after the bright segmented day, that frees us to each other? Or does the infinite space and infinite darkness dwarf and chill us, turning us to seek small human sparks?

Communication—but not for too long. Because good communication is stimulating as black coffee, and just as hard to sleep after. Before we sleep we go out again into the night. We walk up the beach under the stars. And when we are tired of walking, we lie flat on the sand under a bowl of stars. We feel stretched, expanded to take in their compass. They pour into us until we are filled with stars, up to the brim.

This is what one thirsts for, I realize, after the smallness of the day, of work, of details, of intimacy—even of communication, one thirsts for the magnitude and universality of a night full of stars, pouring into one like a fresh tide.

And then at last, from the immensity of interstellar space, we swing down to a particular beach. We walk back to the lights of the cottage glowing from the dark mist of trees. Small, safe, warm and welcoming, we recognize our pinpoint human match-light against the mammoth chaos of the dark. Back again to our good child's sleep.

—ANNE MORROW LINDBERGH

There can be no Friendship where there is no *Freedom*. Friendship loves a *free* Air, and will not be penned up in streight and narrow Enclosures. It will speak *freely*, and *act* so too; and take nothing ill where no ill is meant; nay, where it is, 'twill *easily* forgive, and forget too, upon small Acknowledgments.

—William Penn

34

But, once the realization is accepted that even between the *closest* human beings infinite distances continue to exist, a wonderful living side by side can grow up, if they succeed in loving the distance between them which makes it possible for each to see the other whole and against the wide sky!

—RAINER MARIA RILKE

35

Friendship is essentially a partnership. Also a friend is a second self, so that our consciousness of a friend's existence, when given reality by intercourse with him, makes us more fully conscious of our own existence.

—ARISTOTLE

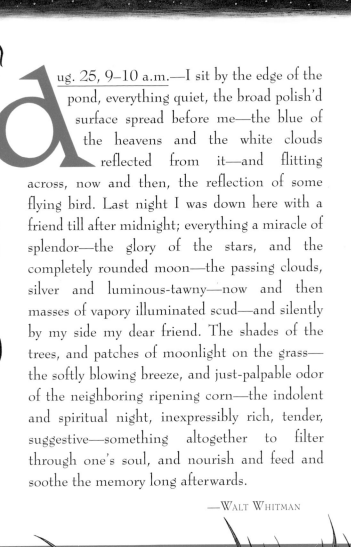

ug. 25, 9–10 a.m.—I sit by the edge of the pond, everything quiet, the broad polish'd surface spread before me—the blue of the heavens and the white clouds reflected from it—and flitting across, now and then, the reflection of some flying bird. Last night I was down here with a friend till after midnight; everything a miracle of splendor—the glory of the stars, and the completely rounded moon—the passing clouds, silver and luminous-tawny—now and then masses of vapory illuminated scud—and silently by my side my dear friend. The shades of the trees, and patches of moonlight on the grass— the softly blowing breeze, and just-palpable odor of the neighboring ripening corn—the indolent and spiritual night, inexpressibly rich, tender, suggestive—something altogether to filter through one's soul, and nourish and feed and soothe the memory long afterwards.

—Walt Whitman

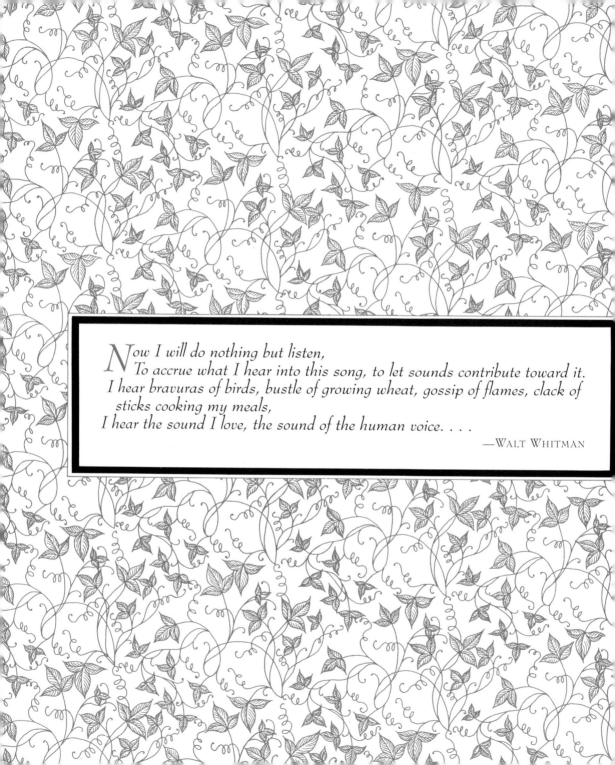

*N*ow I will do nothing but listen,
   To accrue what I hear into this song, to let sounds contribute toward it.
I hear bravuras of birds, bustle of growing wheat, gossip of flames, clack of
   sticks cooking my meals,
I hear the sound I love, the sound of the human voice. . . .

—WALT WHITMAN

Sustenance

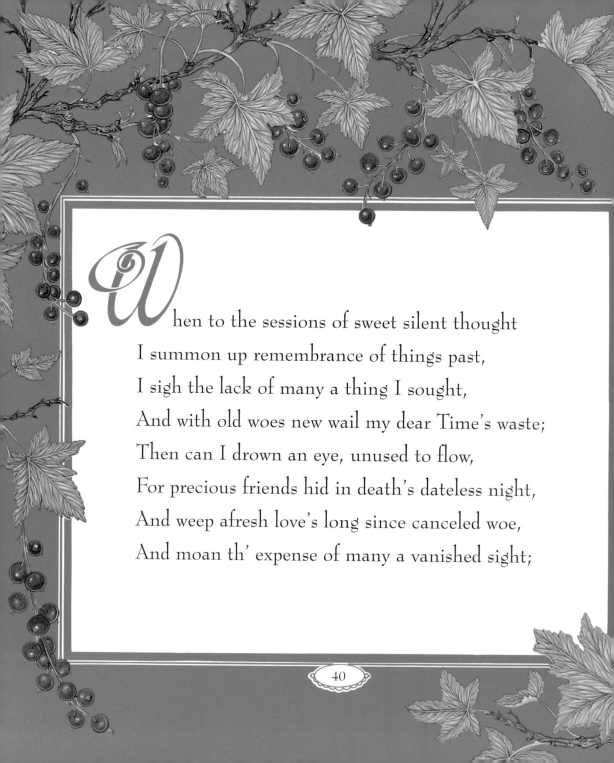

When to the sessions of sweet silent thought

I summon up remembrance of things past,

I sigh the lack of many a thing I sought,

And with old woes new wail my dear Time's waste;

Then can I drown an eye, unused to flow,

For precious friends hid in death's dateless night,

And weep afresh love's long since canceled woe,

And moan th' expense of many a vanished sight;

40

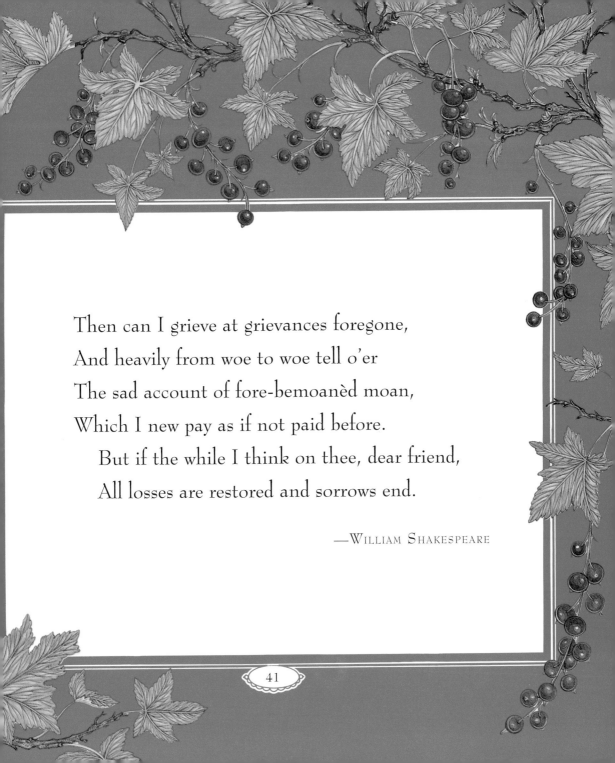

Then can I grieve at grievances foregone,

And heavily from woe to woe tell o'er

The sad account of fore-bemoanèd moan,

Which I new pay as if not paid before.

    But if the while I think on thee, dear friend,

    All losses are restored and sorrows end.

—William Shakespeare

41

ow it came to pass in the days when the judges ruled, that there was a famine in the land. And a certain man of Bethlehem-judah went to sojourn in the country of Moab, he, and his wife, and his two sons.

And the name of the man was Elimelech, and the name of his wife Naomi, and the name of his two sons Mahlon and Chilion, Ephrathites of Bethlehem-judah. And they came into the country of Moab, and continued there.

And Elimelech Naomi's husband died; and she was left, and her two sons.

And they took them wives of the women of Moab; the name of the one was Orpah, and the name of the other Ruth; and they dwelled there about ten years.

And Mahlon and Chilion died also both of them; and the woman was left of her two sons and her husband.

Then she arose with her daughters in law, that she might return from the country of Moab: for she had heard in the country of Moab how that the LORD had visited his people in giving them bread.

Wherefore she went forth out of the place where she was, and her two daughters in law with her; and they went on the way to return unto the land of Judah.

And Naomi said unto her two daughters in law, Go, return each to her mother's house: the LORD deal kindly with you, as ye have dealt with the dead, and with me.

The LORD grant you that ye may find rest, each of you in the house of her husband. Then she kissed them; and they lifted up their voice, and wept.

And they said unto her, Surely we will return with thee unto thy people.

And Naomi said, Turn again, my daughters: why will ye go with me? are there yet any more sons in my womb, that they may be your husbands?

Turn again, my daughters, go your way; for I am too old to have an husband. If I should say, I have hope, if I should have an husband also to night, and should also bear sons;

Would ye tarry for them till they were grown? would ye stay for them from having husbands? nay, my daughters; for it grieveth me much for your sakes that the hand of the LORD is gone out against me.

And they lifted up their voice, and wept again: and Orpah kissed her mother in law; but Ruth clave unto her.

And she said, Behold, thy sister in law is gone back unto her people, and unto her gods: return thou after thy sister in law.

And Ruth said, Intreat me not to leave thee, or to return from following after thee: for whither thou goest, I will go; and where thou lodgest, I will lodge: thy people shall be my people, and thy God my God;

Where thou diest, will I die, and there will I be buried: the LORD do so to me, and more also, if ought but death part thee and me.

—RUTH 1:1–17

43

I shot an arrow into the air,
   It fell to earth, I knew not where;
For so swiftly it flew, the sight
Could not follow it in its flight.

I breathed a song into the air,
It fell to earth, I knew not where;
For, who has sight so keen and strong
That it can follow the flight of song?

Long, long afterward, in an oak
I found the arrow, still unbroke;
And the song, from beginning to end,
I found again in the heart of a friend.

—HENRY WADSWORTH LONGFELLOW

It is only with the heart
that one can see rightly;
what is essential is invisible
to the eye.

—Antoine de Saint-Exupéry

We cannot tell the precise moment when friendship is formed. As in filling a vessel drop by drop, there is at last a drop which makes it run over; so in a series of kindnesses there is at last one which makes the heart run over.

—SAMUEL JOHNSON

Love is like the wild rose-briar,
    Friendship is like the holly-tree—
    The holly is dark when the rose-briar blooms
    But which will bloom most constantly?

    The wild rose-briar is sweet in spring,
    Its summer blossoms scent the air;
    Yet wait till winter comes again
    And who will call the wild-briar fair?

    Then scorn the silly rose-wreath now
    And deck thee with the holly's sheen,
    That when December blights thy brow
    He still may leave thy garland green.

—EMILY BRONTË

47

Of the terrible doubt of appearances,
      Of the uncertainty after all, that we may be deluded,
That may-be reliance and hope are but speculations after all, after all,
That may-be identity beyond the grave is a beautiful fable only,
May-be the things I perceive, the animals, plants, men, hills, shining and flowing waters,
The skies of day and night, colors, densities, forms, may-be these are (as doubtless they are) only apparitions, and the real something has yet to be known,
(How often they dart out of themselves as if to confound me and mock me!
How often I think neither I know, nor any man knows, aught of them,)
May-be seeming to me what they are (as doubtless they indeed but seem) as from my present point of view, and might prove (as of

course they would) nought of what they appear, or nought any-
how, from entirely changed points of view;
To me these and the like of these are curiously answer'd by my
lovers, my dear friends,
When he whom I love travels with me or sits a long while holding
me by the hand,
When the subtle air, the impalpable, the sense that words and
reason hold not, surround us and pervade us,
Then I am charged with untold and untellable wisdom, I am silent,
I require nothing further,
I cannot answer the question of appearances or that of identity
beyond the grave,
But I walk or sit indifferent, I am satisfied,
He ahold of my hand has completely satisfied me.

—WALT WHITMAN

49

Here by the windy docks I stand alone,

But yet companioned. There the vessel goes,

And there my friend goes with it; but the wake

That melts and ebbs between that friend and me

Love's earnest is of Life's all-purposeful

And all-triumphant sailing . . .

—EDWIN ARLINGTON ROBINSON

The end of friendship is a commerce the most strict and homely that can be joined; more strict than any of which we have experience. It is for aid and comfort through all the relations and passages of life and death. It is fit for serene days, and graceful gifts, and country rambles, but also for rough roads and hard fare, shipwreck, poverty, and prosecution. It keeps company with the sallies of the wit and the trances of religion. We are to dignify to each other the daily needs and offices of man's life, and embellish it by courage, wisdom, and unity. It should never fall into something usual and settled, but should be alert and inventive, and add rhyme and reason to what was drudgery.

—RALPH WALDO EMERSON

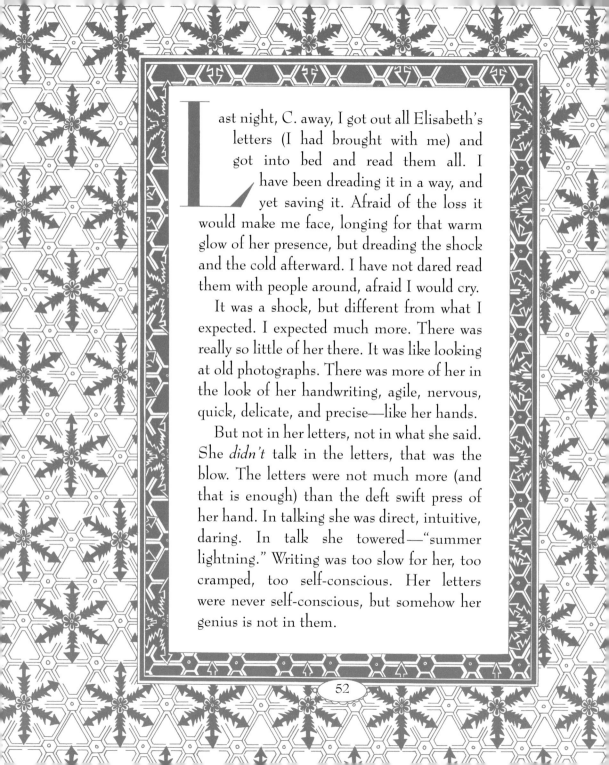

Last night, C. away, I got out all Elisabeth's letters (I had brought with me) and got into bed and read them all. I have been dreading it in a way, and yet saving it. Afraid of the loss it would make me face, longing for that warm glow of her presence, but dreading the shock and the cold afterward. I have not dared read them with people around, afraid I would cry.

It was a shock, but different from what I expected. I expected much more. There was really so little of her there. It was like looking at old photographs. There was more of her in the look of her handwriting, agile, nervous, quick, delicate, and precise—like her hands.

But not in her letters, not in what she said. She *didn't* talk in the letters, that was the blow. The letters were not much more (and that is enough) than the deft swift press of her hand. In talking she was direct, intuitive, daring. In talk she towered—"summer lightning." Writing was too slow for her, too cramped, too self-conscious. Her letters were never self-conscious, but somehow her genius is not in them.

For me the reality of Elisabeth is not there—I found that tonight. It is not in the letters. It is not even in memories . . . very much. But in something undefined in me, in Con, and in Dwight in flashes, something that goes along with me and has—this is the shock—*grown with me*. The Elisabeth I carry around with me every day is much much older than the Elisabeth of those letters. It is she *in me* growing old along with me. Is that possible?

It is something to do with my belief that if you have a person, understand them or perceive them really and deeply at any one instant in their lives, you have them for ever: what they were like as a child, what they will believe in when they are old. It is again in a different dimension the symbol of the crystal: if you could break it up into its component parts, right down to the molecules, each portion would have the same shape—crystalline.

—ANNE MORROW LINDBERGH

53

The best mirror is
an old friend.

—GEORGE HERBERT

54

For there is no friend
    like a sister
In calm or stormy
    weather;
To cheer one on the
    tedious way,
To fetch one if one goes
    astray,
To lift one if one totters
    down,
To strengthen whilst one
    stands.

—Christina Rossetti

A gentleman, or old or young!
   (Bear kindly with my humble lays);
The sacred chorus first was sung
   Upon the first of Christmas days;
The shepherds heard it overhead—
   The joyful angels raised it then:
Glory to Heaven on high, it said,
   And peace on earth to gentle men.

My song, save this, is little worth;
   I lay the weary pen aside,
And wish you health, and love, and mirth,
   As fits the solemn Christmas-tide,
As fits the holy Christmas birth,
   Be this, good friends our carol still,
Be peace on earth, be peace on earth
To men of gentle will.

—WILLIAM MAKEPEACE THACKERAY

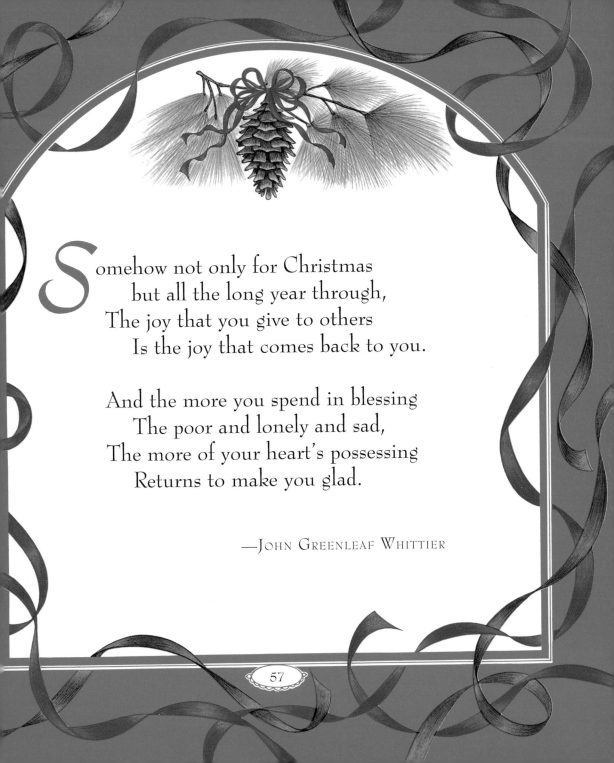

Somehow not only for Christmas
        but all the long year through,
The joy that you give to others
        Is the joy that comes back to you.

And the more you spend in blessing
        The poor and lonely and sad,
The more of your heart's possessing
        Returns to make you glad.

—JOHN GREENLEAF WHITTIER

When a friend calls to me from the road
And slows his horse to a meaning walk,
I don't stand still and look around
On all the hills I haven't hoed,
And shout from where I am, "What is it?"
No, not as there is a time to talk.
I thrust my hoe in the mellow ground,
Blade-end up and five feet tall,
And plod: I go up to the stone wall
For a friendly visit.

—ROBERT FROST

True listening, total concentration on the other, is always a manifestation of love. An essential part of true listening is the discipline of bracketing, the temporary giving up or setting aside of one's own prejudices, frames of reference and desires so as to experience as far as possible the speaker's world from the inside, stepping inside his or her shoes. This unification of speaker and listener is actually an extension and enlargement of ourself, and new knowledge is always gained from this. Moreover, since true listening involves bracketing, a setting aside of the self, it also temporarily involves a total acceptance of the other. Sensing this acceptance, the speaker will feel less and less vulnerable and more and more inclined to open up the inner recesses of his or her mind to the listener. As this happens, speaker and listener begin to appreciate each other more and more, and the duet dance of love is again begun. The energy required for the discipline of bracketing and the focusing of total attention is so great that it can be accomplished only by love, by the will to extend oneself for mutual growth.

—M. Scott Peck

Two are better than one;
because they have a good
reward for their labor.
For if they fall, the one
will lift up his fellow:
but woe unto him that
is alone when he falleth;
for he hath not another
to help him up.

—Ecclesiastes 4:9–10

60

Once we dreamt that
we were strangers.
We wake up to find
that we were dear to
each other.

—RABINDRANATH TAGORE

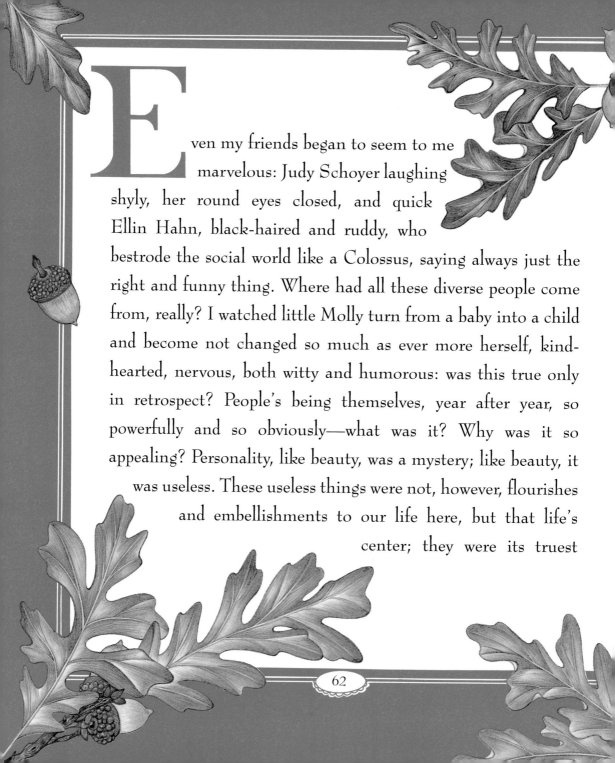

Even my friends began to seem to me marvelous: Judy Schoyer laughing shyly, her round eyes closed, and quick Ellin Hahn, black-haired and ruddy, who bestrode the social world like a Colossus, saying always just the right and funny thing. Where had all these diverse people come from, really? I watched little Molly turn from a baby into a child and become not changed so much as ever more herself, kind-hearted, nervous, both witty and humorous: was this true only in retrospect? People's being themselves, year after year, so powerfully and so obviously—what was it? Why was it so appealing? Personality, like beauty, was a mystery; like beauty, it was useless. These useless things were not, however, flourishes and embellishments to our life here, but that life's center; they were its truest note, the heart of its form, which drew back our thoughts repeatedly. Somewhere between one book and another a child's passive acceptance had slipped away from me also. I could no longer see the world's array as a backdrop to my private play, a dull, neutral backdrop about which I had learned all I needed to know. I had been chipping at the world idly, and had by accident uncovered vast and labyrinthine further worlds within it. I peered in one day, stepped in the next, and soon wandered in deep over my head. Month after month, year after year, the true and brilliant light, and the complex and multifaceted coloration, of this actual, historical, waking world invigorated me. Its vastness extended everywhere I looked, and precisely where I looked, just as forms grew under my gaze as I drew.

—ANNIE DILLARD

*S*ometimes with one I love I fill myself with rage for fear I effuse unreturn'd love,
But now I think there is no unreturn'd love, the pay is certain one way or
another,
(I loved a certain person ardently and my love was not return'd,
Yet out of that I have written these songs.)

—WALT WHITMAN

Changes

There is no greater
desert or wilderness
than to be without
true friends.

—Francis Bacon

66

Grief can take care of itself, but to get the full value of a joy you must have somebody to divide it with.

—MARK TWAIN

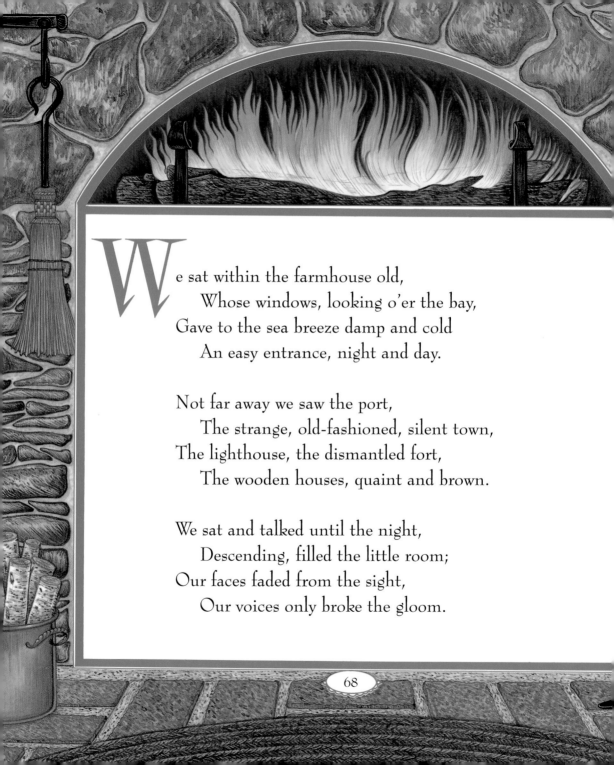

We sat within the farmhouse old,
    Whose windows, looking o'er the bay,
Gave to the sea breeze damp and cold
    An easy entrance, night and day.

Not far away we saw the port,
    The strange, old-fashioned, silent town,
The lighthouse, the dismantled fort,
    The wooden houses, quaint and brown.

We sat and talked until the night,
    Descending, filled the little room;
Our faces faded from the sight,
    Our voices only broke the gloom.

We spake of many a vanished scene,
　　Of what we once had thought and said,
Of what had been, and might have been,
　　And who was changed, and who was dead;

And all that fills the hearts of friends,
　　When first they feel, with secret pain,
Their lives henceforth have separate ends,
　　And never can be one again;

The first slight swerving of the heart,
　　That words are powerless to express,
And leave it still unsaid in part,
　　Or say it in too great excess.

The very tones in which we spake
    Had something strange, I could but mark;
The leaves of memory seemed to make
    A mournful rustling in the dark.

Oft died the words upon our lips,
    As suddenly, from out the fire
Built of the wreck of stranded ships,
    The flames would leap and then expire.

And, as their splendor flashed and failed,
    We thought of wrecks upon the main,
Of ships dismasted, that were hailed
    And sent no answer back again.

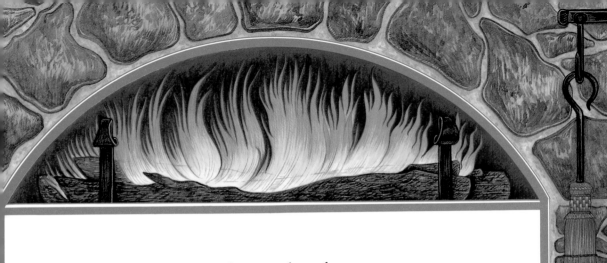

The windows, rattling in their frames,
    The ocean, roaring up the beach,
The gusty blast, the bickering flames,
    All mingled vaguely in our speech;

Until they made themselves a part
    Of fancies floating through the brain,
The long-lost ventures of the heart,
    That send no answers back again.

O flames that glowed! O hearts that yearned!
    They were indeed too much akin,
The driftwood fire without that burned,
    The thoughts that burned and glowed within.

—HENRY WADSWORTH LONGFELLOW

Anger makes
A person forget
This world, the next worlds,
Other people,
And himself.

—*A Zen Harvest*

72

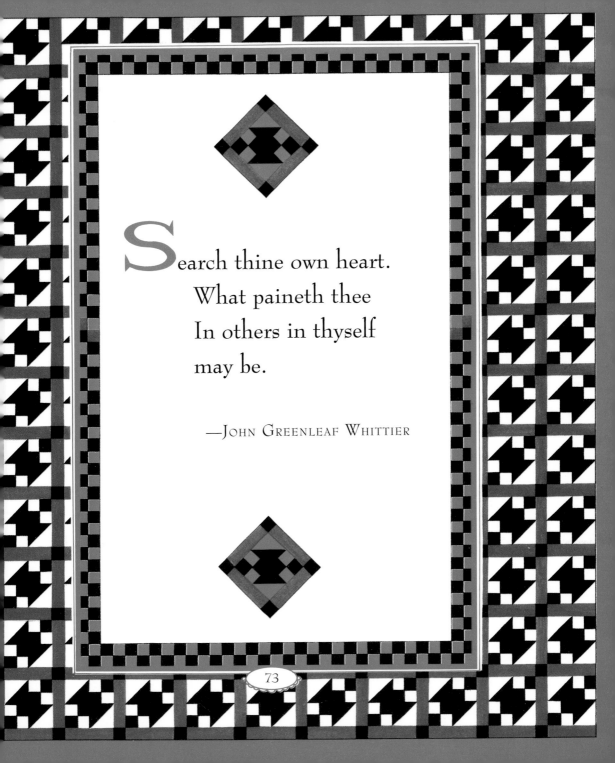

Search thine own heart.
What paineth thee
In others in thyself
may be.

—JOHN GREENLEAF WHITTIER

As I wandered over those rough pastures, I had the good luck to stumble upon a bit of the first road that went from Black Hawk out to the north country; to my grandfather's farm, then on to the Shimerdas' and to the Norwegian settlement. Everywhere else it had been ploughed under when the highways were surveyed; this half-mile or so within the pasture fence was all that was left of that old road which used to run like a wild thing across the open prairie, clinging to the high places and circling and doubling like a rabbit before the hounds.

On the level land the tracks had almost disappeared—were mere shadings in the grass, and a stranger would not have noticed them. But wherever the road had crossed a draw, it was easy to find. The rains had made channels of the wheel-ruts and washed them so deeply that the sod had never healed over them. They looked like gashes torn by a grizzly's claws, on the slopes where the farm-wagons used to lurch up out of the hollows with

a pull that brought curling muscles on the smooth hips of the horses. I sat down and watched the haystacks turn rosy in the slanting sunlight.

This was the road over which Ántonia and I came on that night when we got off the train at Black Hawk and were bedded down in the straw, wondering children, being taken we knew not whither. I had only to close my eyes to hear the rumbling of the wagons in the dark, and to be again overcome by that obliterating strangeness. The feelings of that night were so near that I could reach out and touch them with my hand. I had the sense of coming home to myself, and of having found out what a little circle man's experience is. For Ántonia and for me, this had been the road of Destiny; had taken us to those early accidents of fortune which predetermined for us all that we can ever be. Now I understood that the same road was to bring us together again. Whatever we had missed, we possessed together the precious, the incommunicable past.

—WILLA CATHER

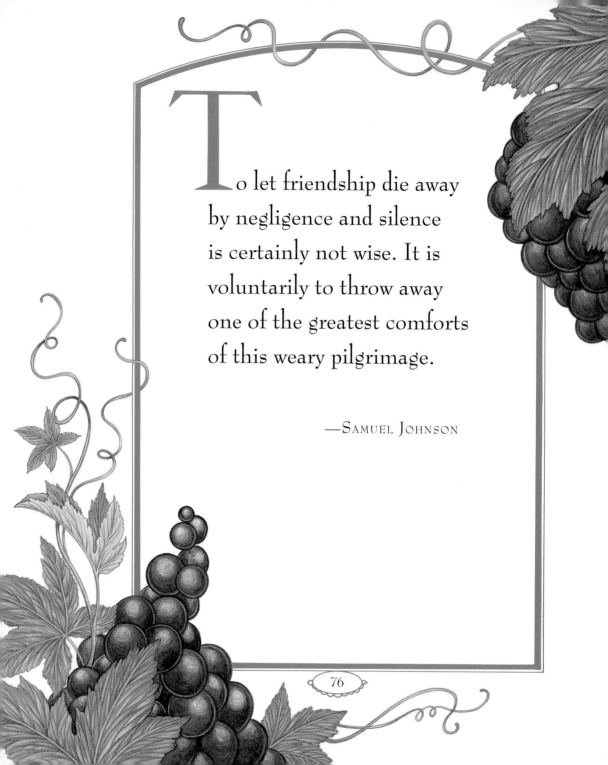

To let friendship die away
by negligence and silence
is certainly not wise. It is
voluntarily to throw away
one of the greatest comforts
of this weary pilgrimage.

—SAMUEL JOHNSON

When the weariness of the road is upon me, and the thirst of the sultry day; when the ghostly hours of the dusk throw their shadows across my life, then I cry out not for your voice only, my friend, but for your touch.

There is an anguish in my heart for the burden of its riches not given to you.

Put out your hand through the night, let me hold it and fill it and keep it; let me feel its touch along the lengthening stretch of my loneliness.

—RABINDRANATH TAGORE

Now goes under, and I watch it go under, the sun
    That will not rise again.
Today has seen the setting, in your eyes cold and senseless
    as the sea,
Of friendship better than bread, and of bright charity
That lifts a man a little above the beasts that run.

That this could be!
That I should live to see
Most vulgar Pride, that stale obstreperous clown,
So fitted out with purple robe and crown
To stand among his betters! Face to face
With outraged me in this once holy place,
Where Wisdom was a favoured guest and hunted

Truth was harboured out of danger,
He bulks enthroned, a lewd, an insupportable stranger!

I would have sworn, indeed I swore it:
The hills may shift, the waters may decline,
Winter may twist the stem from the twig that bore it,
But never your love from me, your hand from mine.

Now goes under the sun, and I watch it go under.
Farewell, sweet light, great wonder!
You, too, farewell,—but fare not well enough to dream
You have done wisely to invite the night before the darkness
    came.

—EDNA ST. VINCENT MILLAY

Heart! We will forget him!
You and I—tonight!
You may forget the
    warmth he gave—
I will forget the light!

When you have done,
    pray tell me
That I may straight begin!
Haste! lest while you're
    lagging
I remember him!

—EMILY DICKINSON

80

I held a Jewel in my fingers—
And went to sleep—
The day was warm, and
    winds were prosy—
I said " 'Twill keep"—

I woke—and chid my
    honest fingers,
The Gem was gone—
And now, an Amethyst
    remembrance
Is all I own—

—EMILY DICKINSON

81

ow much you have endured of storm
Among sweet summer flowers!
The black hail falls so hard to do us harm
In my dark hours.

Though friendship is not quick to burn,
It is explosive stuff;
The edge of our awareness is so keen
A word is enough.

Clouds rise up from the blue

And darken the sky,

And we are tossed about from false to true

Not knowing why.

After this violence is over

I turn my life, my art,

Round and around to discover

The fault in my heart—

What breeds this cruel weather,

Why tensions grow;

And when we have achieved so much together,

What breaks the flow.

God help us, friendship is aware

That where we fail we learn;

Tossed on a temperament, I meet you there

At every turn.

In this kaleidoscope

Of work and complex living,

For years you buttressed and enlivened hope,

Laid balm on grieving.

After the angry cloud has broken

I know what you are—

How love renews itself, spoken, unspoken,

Cool as the morning star.

—MAY SARTON

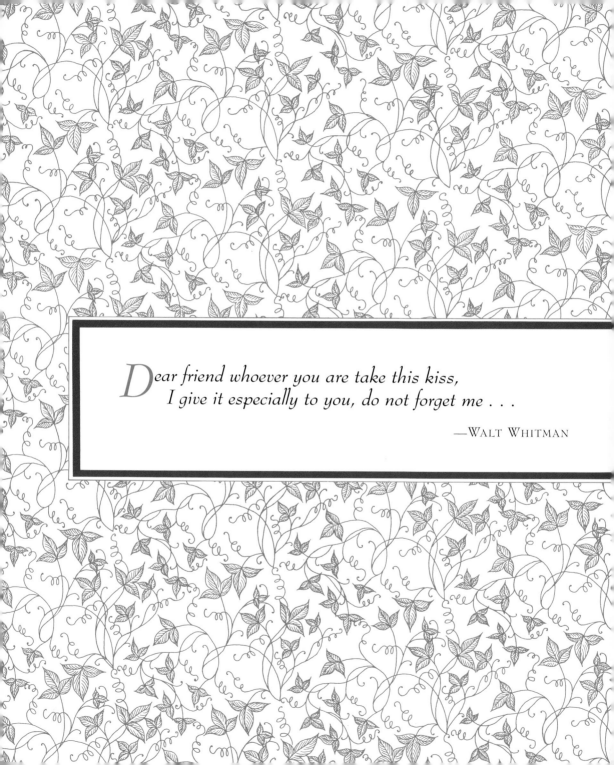

Dear friend whoever you are take this kiss,
I give it especially to you, do not forget me . . .

—WALT WHITMAN

The real marriage of true minds is for any two people to possess a sense of humour or irony pitched in exactly the same key, so that their joint glances at any subject cross like interarching searchlights.

—EDITH WHARTON

Let me not to the marriage of true minds
     Admit impediments; love is not love
Which alters when it alteration finds,
Or bends with the remover to remove.
O, no, it is an ever-fixèd mark
That looks on tempests and is never shaken;
It is the star to every wandering bark,
Whose worth's unknown, although his height
   be taken.
Love's not Time's fool, though rosy lips and
   cheeks
Within his bending sickle's compass come;
Love alters not with his brief hours and weeks,
But bears it out even to the edge of doom.
   If this be error and upon me proved,
   I never writ, nor no man ever loved.

—WILLIAM SHAKESPEARE

89

There are two elements that go to the composition of friendship, each so sovereign that I can detect no superiority in either, no reason why either should be first named. One is Truth. A friend is a person with whom I may be sincere. Before him I may think aloud. I am arrived at last in the presence of a man so real and equal, that I may drop even those undermost garments of dissimulation, courtesy, and second thought, which men never put off, and may deal with him with the simplicity and wholeness with which one chemical atom meets another. . . .

The other element of friendship is tenderness. We are holden to men by every sort of tie, by blood, by pride, by fear, by hope, by lucre, by lust, by hate, by admiration, by every circumstance and badge and trifle, but we can scarce believe that so much character can subsist in another as to draw us by love. Can another be so blessed, and we so pure, that we can offer him tenderness? When a man becomes dear to me, I have touched the goal of fortune.

—Ralph Waldo Emerson

One cannot always tell what it is that keeps us shut in, confines us, seems to bury us; nevertheless, one feels certain barriers, certain gates, certain walls. Is all this imagination, fantasy? I don't think so. And one asks, "My God! is it for long, is it forever, is it for all eternity?"

Do you know what frees one from this captivity? It is every deep serious affection. Being friends, being brothers, love, that is what opens the prison by some supreme power, by some magic force. Without this, one remains in prison. Where sympathy is renewed, life is restored.

—Vincent van Gogh

*H*ad I the heavens' embroidered cloths,
  Enwrought with golden and silver light,
  The blue and the dim and the dark cloths
  Of night and light and the half-light,
  I would spread the cloths under your feet:
  But I, being poor, have only my dreams;
  I have spread my dreams under your feet;
  Tread softly because you tread on my dreams.

—W. B. YEATS

$\mathcal{A}$t the last, tenderly,
   From the walls of the powerful fortress'd house,
From the clasp of the knitted locks, from the keep of the well-
   closed doors,
Let me be wafted.

Let me glide noiselessly forth;
With the key of softness unlock the locks—with a whisper,
Set ope the doors O soul.

Tenderly—be not impatient,
(Strong is your hold O mortal flesh,
Strong is your hold O love.)

—WALT WHITMAN

Not for me is the love that knows no restraint, but like the foaming wine that having burst its vessel in a moment would run to waste.

Send me the love which is cool and pure like your rain that blesses the thirsty earth and fills the homely earthen jars.

Send me the love that would soak down into the centre of being, and from there would spread like the unseen sap through the branching tree of life, giving birth to fruits and flowers.

Send me the love that keeps the heart still with the fulness of peace.

—Rabindranath Tagore

Familiar acts are beautiful
Through love. . . .

—Percy Bysshe Shelley

95

And a woman who held a babe against her bosom said, Speak to us of Children.

And he said:

Your children are not your children.

They are the sons and daughters of Life's longing for itself.

They come through you but not from you,

And though they are with you yet they belong not to you.

You may give them your love but not your thoughts,

For they have their own thoughts.

You may house their bodies but not their souls,

For their souls dwell in the house of to-morrow, which you cannot visit, not even in your dreams.

You may strive to be like them, but seek not to
 make them like you.
For life goes not backward nor tarries with
 yesterday.
You are the bows from which your children as
 living arrows are sent forth.
The archer sees the mark upon the path of the
 infinite, and He bends you with His might
 that His arrows may go swift and far.
Let your bending in the Archer's hand be for
 gladness;
For even as He loves the arrow that flies, so He
 loves also the bow that is stable.

—KAHLIL GIBRAN

Mother, I love you so.
Said the child, I love
you more than I know.
She laid her head on
her mother's arm,
And the love between
them kept them warm.

—STEVIE SMITH

98

Love alone is capable of uniting living beings in a such a way as to complete and fulfill them, for it alone takes them and joins them by what is deepest in themselves.

—Pierre Teilhard de Chardin

99

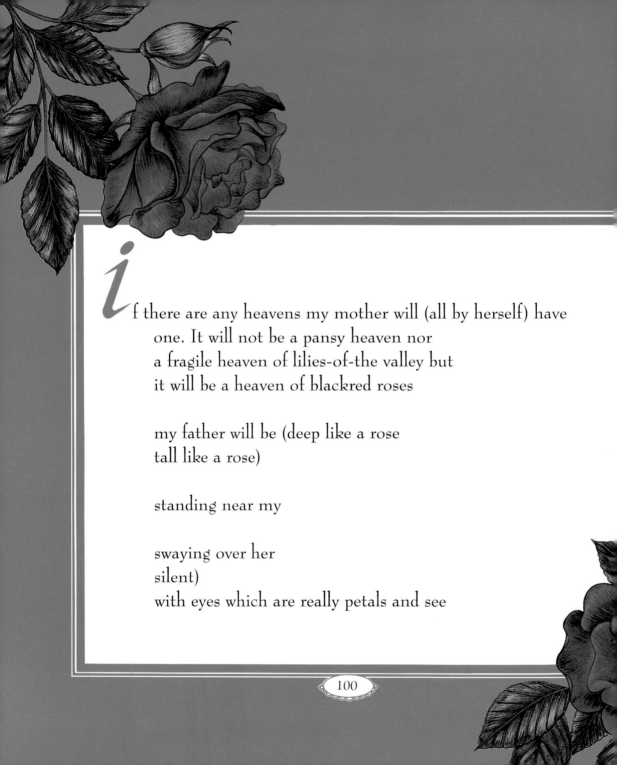

*i*f there are any heavens my mother will (all by herself) have
      one. It will not be a pansy heaven nor
      a fragile heaven of lilies-of-the valley but
      it will be a heaven of blackred roses

      my father will be (deep like a rose
      tall like a rose)

      standing near my

      swaying over her
      silent)
      with eyes which are really petals and see

nothing with the face of a poet really which
is a flower and not a face with
hands
which whisper
This is my beloved my

                (suddenly in sunlight

he will bow,

& the whole garden will bow)

—E. E. CUMMINGS

My mother and I were double-sided people, often at cross-purposes. She felt her responsibilities toward me keenly and tried to make a woman of me (she must have despaired of the task, since I was indolent by nature and spent most of my time listening to radio serials and reading). What she taught was not necessarily what I learned. Her spoken lessons were just what any good mother of the 1940s was teaching her daughter. But what she really wanted me to know I learned by going to the movies and the beauty parlor with her and through what I overheard her saying to my aunt as they sewed. I listened well. I was a better student than she thought. But one of the things she most wanted me to learn was something I never quite absorbed: dissimulate. Hide. Never let anybody know what your true feelings are. Unlike that of the belle, however, her purpose was defensive rather than predatory. . . .

I don't know how many women like her are still left. I don't know whether her doctrine is the right one—if that is the word to apply to her beliefs. She would have understood the things that many women are now determined to gain—titles, power, high salaries, the right to define themselves by male standards of success. She certainly knew firsthand why women need an education and good salaries, and it never occurred to her that they need to apologize for working outside the home, or in it either.

But the idea that happiness is likely to result from having a succession of lovers she would have thought silly. To exchange the certainties of the kitchen and the

laundry room for the risky pleasures of the boudoir would have struck her as a dubious bargain. She didn't believe that feminine liberation had anything to do with sex but rather with paychecks.

Nor could she ever have agreed that housework is degrading drudgery that ought to be sloughed off on the maid, or that children drag a woman down. In fact, the whole notion that an assiduous fussing over one's own self, an endless vigil over one's own feelings and moods, an elaborate absorption in one's own body could be a source of satisfaction or a way of life would have astounded her. I think she would have gotten a good laugh over the recent discovery of certain avant-garde women that the experience of having a baby and raising it is, after all, worthwhile. But she wouldn't have laughed too hard. She never was the sort to downgrade other people's accomplishments.

She was one of the mass of women who work as housewives or as underpaid help in the outside world. Urban, educated feminists tend to dislike them for being regressive and reactionary and a passel of ingrates. I myself have become some sort of urban, educated feminist, and my mother and I are still at cross-purposes. Particularly since my daughters were born, she has whispered in my ear each night as I slept, trying to remake me in her image. I battle her off as well as I can, but she touches me still, and I love her. I would not want my children to grow up without knowing what their grandmother thought.

—Shirley Abbott

Love is a great thing,
a great good in every
wise: it alone maketh
light every heavy thing
and beareth evenly
every uneven thing.

—Thomas à Kempis

104

For one human being
to love another:
that is perhaps the
hardest of all our
tasks, the ultimate,
the last test and
proof, the work for
which all other
work is but
preparation.

—RAINER MARIA RILKE

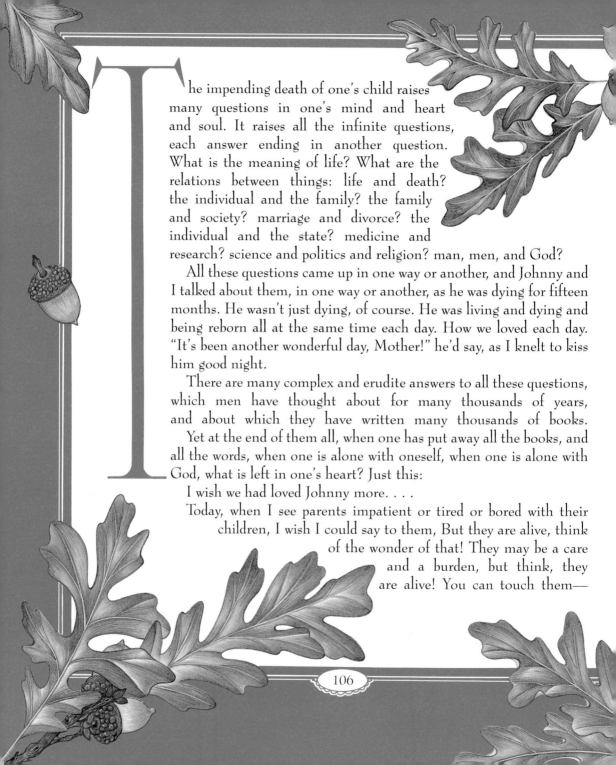

The impending death of one's child raises many questions in one's mind and heart and soul. It raises all the infinite questions, each answer ending in another question. What is the meaning of life? What are the relations between things: life and death? the individual and the family? the family and society? marriage and divorce? the individual and the state? medicine and research? science and politics and religion? man, men, and God?

All these questions came up in one way or another, and Johnny and I talked about them, in one way or another, as he was dying for fifteen months. He wasn't just dying, of course. He was living and dying and being reborn all at the same time each day. How we loved each day. "It's been another wonderful day, Mother!" he'd say, as I knelt to kiss him good night.

There are many complex and erudite answers to all these questions, which men have thought about for many thousands of years, and about which they have written many thousands of books.

Yet at the end of them all, when one has put away all the books, and all the words, when one is alone with oneself, when one is alone with God, what is left in one's heart? Just this:

I wish we had loved Johnny more. . . .

Today, when I see parents impatient or tired or bored with their children, I wish I could say to them, But they are alive, think of the wonder of that! They may be a care and a burden, but think, they are alive! You can touch them—

106

what a miracle! You don't have to hold back sudden tears when you see just a headline about the Yale–Harvard game because you know your boy will never see the Yale–Harvard game, never see the house in Paris he was born in, never bring home his girl, and you will not hand down your jewels to his bride and will have no grandchildren to play with and spoil. Your sons and daughters are live. Think of that—not dead but alive! Exult and sing.

All parents who have lost a child will feel what I mean. Others, luckily, cannot. But I hope they will embrace them with a little added rapture and a keener awareness of joy.

I wish we had loved Johnny more when he was alive. Of course we loved Johnny very much. Johnny knew that. Everybody knew it. Loving Johnny more. What does it mean? What can it mean, now?

Parents all over the earth who lost sons in the war have felt this kind of question, and sought an answer. To me, it means loving life more, being more aware of life, of one's fellow human beings, of the earth.

It means obliterating, in a curious but real way, the ideas of evil and hate and the enemy, and transmuting them, with the alchemy of suffering, into ideas of clarity and charity.

It means caring more and more about other people, at home and abroad, all over the earth. It means caring more about God.

I hope we can love Johnny more and more till we too die, and leave behind us, as he did, the love of love, the love of life.

—FRANCES GUNTHER

Acknowledgments

Grateful acknowledgment is made for permission to reprint the following copyrighted works:

"Revelation" and "A Time to Talk" by Robert Frost, from *The Poetry of Robert Frost*, edited by Edward Connery Lathem, published by Henry Holt & Co., Inc., 1969. Copyright 1944, © 1962 by Robert Frost. Copyright 1916, 1934, © 1969 by Henry Holt and Company, Inc. Reprinted by permission of Henry Holt and Company, Inc.

Selections from *A Zen Harvest: Japanese Folk Zen Sayings*, compiled and translated by Soigu Shigematsu. Copyright © 1988 by Soigu Shigematsu. Reprinted by permission of North Point Press, a division of Farrar, Straus & Giroux.

Excerpts from *The Art of Loving* by Erich Fromm. Copyright © 1956 by Erich Fromm. Copyright renewed. Reprinted by permission of HarperCollins Publishers, Inc.

Excerpt from *Discovery of a Father* by Sherwood Anderson. Reprinted by permission of Harold Ober Associates, Incorporated. Copyright 1939 by The Reader's Digest. Copyright renewed 1966 by Eleanor Copenhauer Anderson.

Excerpt from *When All You've Ever Wanted Isn't Enough* by Harold Kushner. Copyright © 1986 by Kushner Enterprises, Inc. Reprinted by permission of Simon & Schuster, Inc.

Excerpts from *The Prophet* by Kahlil Gibran. Copyright 1923 by Kahlil Gibran and renewed 1951 by Administrators C.T.A. of Kahlil Gibran Estate and Mary G. Gibran. Reprinted by permission of Alfred A. Knopf, Inc.

Excerpt from *Modeling My Life* by Janet Scudder, published by Harcourt, Brace & Co., 1925.

Excerpt from *A Gift from the Sea* by Anne Morrow Lindbergh. Copyright © 1955 by Anne Morrow Lindbergh. Reprinted by permission of Pantheon Books, a division of Random House, Inc.